JAMES HOPE MOULTON

11th October 1863—7th April 1917

WIPF & STOCK · Eugene, Oregon

Wipf and Stock Publishers
199 W 8th Ave, Suite 3
Eugene, OR 97401

James Hope Moulton
11th October 1863—7th April 1917
By Moulton, Harold K.
Copyright©1963 Methodist Publishing - Epworth Press
ISBN 13: 978-1-5326-3835-0
Publication date 7/27/2017
Previously published by Epworth Press, 1963

Acknowledgements

I T S E E M E D right that, on the occasion of the centenary of his birth, the present generation should be reminded of James Hope Moulton.

Fortunately a number of his old friends are still with us, and I am most deeply grateful to those who have drawn on their memory and their abiding admiration and affection in order to contribute to this book :

The Rev. Dr W. F. Lofthouse, now in his nineties, for many years Theological Tutor at Handsworth College;

Mrs G. Elsie Harrison, daughter of the Rev. Dr J. S. Simon and widow of the Rev. Dr A. W. Harrison, both colleagues of my father at Didsbury College;

The Revs. A. H. Bray, Assistant Tutor, Didsbury, 1912-14; J. H. Bodgener, Didsbury, 1905-08; J. O. Cochran, Didsbury, 1908-11;

Mrs Doris Hurst, a student of my father at Manchester University;

The Rev. Frank Hart, Methodist Chaplain in Bombay during my father's time there;

Mrs Helen Hope Hollings, my sister.

Their recollections confirm one another remarkably, and paint a picture that no single pen can do.

11th October 1963   HAROLD K. MOULTON

Contents

Foreword

THE ONLY reason why I should have the honour of writing this Foreword is the two-fold one : that I knew James Hope Moulton when he was still living with his younger brother under his father's roof at the headmaster's house of The Leys School; and that I was more or less in touch with him continuously till the tragedy and triumph of his return from India in the first world war.

For some reason I was sent as a supply from Richmond College to The Leys School in 1896; a solemn occasion for me, for his father was a great New Testament scholar. His *Concordance to the Greek Testament* was then appearing, and he held the destinies of the Probationers in his hands. But I found myself surprisingly at home; James Hope was already making for himself a name in the world of scholarship, and the father and both his sons playfully sparred together as equals. I had known nothing like it. An undergraduate at Oxford, especially if he is interested in religion, and even theology, has some opportunity for meeting prominent people; but this was a place where knowledge, thought, piety and connexional influence all went together. To understand the atmosphere in which James Hope grew up, one story (a kind of family joke) is worth repeating. Dr W. F. Moulton was dining one evening with Bishop Lightfoot; they had been fellow-revisers of the New Testament. A lady at the table rather innocently asked the Bishop if he did not find it hard to mix with so varied a crowd, 'those dissenters, for example'. 'Not in the least,' replied the Bishop; 'one of my old colleagues is sitting near to you at the table this evening.'

James Hope was a Cambridge man to the finger-tips. The founder of Wesley House at Cambridge was asked why he chose Cambridge and not Oxford—'Think of John

Wesley himself.' 'I had always intended that the house should be at Cambridge; I have noticed that the Oxford men in our ministry have such a lot of side.' Whatever might be said about 'those Oxford fellows', James Hope had the true scholar's gift: 'gladly would he learn, and gladly teach'.

Few would think of him today as a leader in a body of revolutionaries. But it so happened that in the early years of this century a band of young Methodists was formed to promote the study of social service, under the wise but daring guidance of Samuel Keeble. Those were the days in which only one thing was worse than to call oneself a democrat, and that was to invite the devastating question 'Are you a socialist?' The question was boldly answered by men like Ensor Walters, Harry Bisseker, Henry Carter, Maldwyn Hughes and, one who out-lived most of his generation, J. E. Rattenbury. It would perhaps be too much to find a parallel in the early days of the Oxford Movement, when the younger men like John Henry Newman found that they could rely on the wise caution of the elderly E. B. Pusey. But the younger Methodists found that they had the unlooked for support of James Hope and Scott Lidgett. They knew that they had the loyalty of men like Frank Richards behind them, and they could all point to Hugh Price Hughes. At one time the Union was almost split by the demand of some of its members for a more definite socialist programme. The motto of the Union was 'See and serve'. James Hope was one of what we should now call the 'leftist' party, and he made the suggestion, agreed to by all, that the extremer members like himself should be known as the 'Sigma' club—'sigma' being the first letter of 'socialist'. The Union hardly survived the first world war, but Methodism has been a different thing ever since. One feels the difference between the old Temperance Committee and the 'Christian Citizenship Movement' today.

James Hope always felt that in the world of scholarship a man should never say what he was not prepared to defend; but, if it was a matter of opinion, he would ask 'If you believe it true, why not say so?' During the war he travelled to India for the Y.M.C.A. with his friend Rendel Harris. Their ship was torpedoed on the way home. James Hope died from exposure in the open boat; Harris was nursed back into safety by two ladies who, between their cigarettes, gave him all he needed. 'You have done so much for me,' he said, 'that you must come to my house; and you shall smoke in every room; and,' he added, 'they did.' James Hope would have said the same thing.

Most men who think of him now will remember him as the Greek Testament tutor at Didsbury College. His fellowship at King's, Cambridge, is almost forgotten. At Didsbury he had an excellent Old Testament colleague, C. L. Bedale, also a war casualty; and a man whom he had specially trained, W. F. Howard, who subsequently married Bedale's sister, and later on held a tutorship of far-reaching influence at Handsworth. All his time at Didsbury, James Hope was working at a new and quite re-written edition of Winer's *New Testament Grammar*, the earlier edition of which James Hope's father had translated. I, at that time a colleague of Howard's, had unrivalled opportunity of seeing the labour of love with which James Hope produced the two volumes that came from his pen, and the wealth of material which Howard as lovingly used for the remainder. James Hope was indeed a pioneer in the study of the papyri. *From Egyptian Rubbish Heaps* was one of his titles; and no one who knew him could doubt the energy with which he would have thrown himself into the study of the Qumran documents.

A true Cambridge man, he was always suspicious of the Oxford belief in 'Greats'; and it was a real grief when his elder son Ralph showed an interest in philosophy, which he could not share himself. But the rift was not as deep as might have appeared. James Hope's work involved a large knowledge of the 'semantics' (using the word in its wider sense), as Howard found when he was taking over the Greek Testament work; and Ralph solaced his leisure, while he was waiting to go overseas, by studying Arabic. Although James Hope never thought of himself as a philosopher, no one could do the work on Zoroaster which he accomplished without a large knowledge of the philosophic issues raised by that great religion; nor is it possible to write a grammar of any language, least of all the *Koine* as used by the New Testament writers, without being something of a philosopher himself. Though one should say, as James Hope said of himself, that he fought shy of theology, the division between the different objects of study today is increasingly difficult to understand.

But the few notes in these pages may, to my mind, be best summed up by a reference to what might be called one of his more popular devotional books, *The Neglected Sacrament*. In these days of 'liturgiological' studies, one can imagine James Hope, whose friendship with Cliff College never died down, saying to himself, 'Let us get away for a time to what was assuredly a sacramental act, introduced with so much care by the Fourth Evangelist who never referred in so many words to the institution of the eucharist as "the Lord's Supper". Can we be sure that the Evangelist did not regard the foot-washing as being as important as the eucharist itself? Can the breaking of the bread, the pouring of the wine, have any value apart from the act which follows? At all events, to take the life of Jesus into our own bodies must be to enshrine the example which he left us in our hearts "You are my disciples if ye do to each other as I have done to you". Is the eating and drinking more than a mockery, unless we do all that is typified by the foot-washing?' There speaks the real James Hope. No one could ever accuse him of treating the eucharist as small or trivial. But we do not live to eat; we eat to live. To think that all that is required of us is to 'make our communion' so many times a year, is sheer falsehood; as false as to think that to Jesus, on that memorable occasion, unity meant the discovery of a formula for the ministry which should satisfy all the churches which exist today. James Hope knew what He meant by the unity of the disciples with one another in their Master.

And so he has passed from us. We have forgotten other leaders; we shall doubtless in time forget him. But his spirit will live on with us. To all who have known the humility of sound learning, of the study of the word from the pebble on the shore to the mountain-top, and who have felt his selfless devotion to the truth as it is in Jesus, he will still speak. Like all who have admired him, with his body left near 'the great vision of the guarded mount', he will 'twitch his mantle blue'. 'For Lycidas our sorrow is not dead'; and we too may tomorrow find our way to 'fresh woods and pastures new'.

> Jesus, the first and last,
> On Thee my soul is cast.

W. F. LOFTHOUSE

James Hope Moulton

IN THE NATURE of things it can never be easy for a son to write of his father. There is a generation between them. His words cannot—perhaps should not—be entirely objective. He may be too personal, or lean over backwards to be too little so.

Yet I am singularly fortunate. My father was, by common consent of all who knew him, a man great in scholarship, in Christian character, and in achievement and influence. There are no sides to take in writing about him. Further, all who have shown him to me—my uncle in his biography of his brother, his old friends and students (some of whom testify to him in this book), the tributes that were written about him at his death—have given me, a boy of twelve when I last saw him and only thirteen when he died, an understanding of him such as few in such circumstances could ever have hoped to receive. Most of all, his own writings have shown me what he was like, by the range and depth of their scholarship, their vividness and warmth, their crusading for the truth, their humble Christian goodness. His books can do this for all, but some of us have also the weekly circular letters that he wrote for eighteen months from India, nearly a million words of them, full of wisdom, wit, interestedness, activities, caring for others, eagerness for the spread of the Gospel. Though not in any technical sense confidential, they were meant for an intimate circle of relatives and close friends, and I cannot be grateful enough for the way in which they have opened his mind and heart to me, and given me, when I was mature enough to receive it, what I should otherwise have lost altogether.

Besides these various communications from without, would it be fanciful or arrogant to say that I feel I know him a little 'in my bones', and that there is something in heredity, however muted the characteristics in the next generation may be? Of two things I am sure: I am very proud to be his son—and always humbled.

My father was born at Richmond College a hundred years ago, on 11th October 1863. His father, William F. Moulton, was Classical Tutor there at the time, but the Methodist ancestry of the family went back another four generations to John Bakewell, one of Wesley's preachers and author of 'Hail, thou once despised Jesus'. His daughter married a schoolmaster named Egan, whose name has been continued in the family, and their daughter married William Moulton, who was converted under Methodism and entered the Methodist ministry in 1794. Their son, James Egan Moulton the first, followed in his father's footsteps, and so did two of the next generation: the eldest son, William Fiddian, and his brother, James Egan the second, for forty years a missionary in Tonga. My father was thus a sixth generation Methodist and a fourth generation minister. My own ministry continues the father and son succession, stretching back now for nearly a hundred and seventy years.

Other relationships besides the direct line may just be mentioned. In addition to Moulton of Tonga, my father had two uncles: John Fletcher Moulton (named after Fletcher of Madeley) who became a Lord Justice of Appeal, and after whom the Moulton Hall at Kingswood is called; and Richard Green Moulton, for many years Professor of English in Chicago and editor of The Modern Reader's Bible, the pioneer of all modern Bible arrangements. By marriage at various points Fiddians, Hopes, Osborns and Keelings came into the family, so that I have—I believe— the blood of nine Methodist ministers in my veins.

My father and his younger brother, who had his father's

names, were thus steeped in Methodism both by heredity and by environment. The physical environment was changed when my father was only eleven, because my grandfather was transferred in 1875 to Cambridge, to found The Leys School. For the next seven years James Hope Moulton was a pupil there. Before he was fifteen he was reciting the Greek Verse welcome at Speech Day, appearing in the prize lists, and contributing to the school magazine on such subjects as 'Milton's Minor Poems' (an essay spread over several numbers), and 'Comets'. This latter essay, written just after he reached fifteen, is perfectly at home in the technicalities of astronomy, a subject in which he maintained a lifelong interest. The magazine over the next few years gives regular evidence of maturing powers : football and athletics, with special reference to his speed; senior prefect for two years; sixth in the Kingdom in London Matriculation, and finally a scholarship in Classics at King's College, Cambridge.

There the same record continues at an advanced level : a double first in the Classical Tripos, the University Lacrosse team in all four of his undergraduate years, the Chancellor's Gold Medal for a full length poem on Vasco da Gama, and a Fellowship at King's in 1888, the first Cambridge Fellowship to be awarded to a Methodist minister. Academic studies were also continued in connection with London University, leading to an M.A. with another Gold Medal, and to a D.Lit. in 1901.

From King's he returned to The Leys, this time as a master, but lecturing also in Classics to the women's colleges in Cambridge. He was offered a mastership at Harrow, but declined it.

Brilliant though this academic record was, however, it was far from being the whole of his life. Along with his scholarship went a religion that was characteristic of Methodism

14

at its best : personal, evangelistic and social. If it might have been expected that, with his background, he would naturally turn towards the ordained ministry, that is by no means always the case. There are many who turn against their background, and many others who feel called to serve the Church as laymen.

My father's diary tells both of his own conversion and of his being used to bring others to Christ, but he was not content simply to make his inherited religion his own. He also was sure of his call to the ministry, following by personal conviction in the footsteps of his forbears. He was accepted as a probationer in 1886 and designated to assist his father at The Leys. He was ordained in 1890 at the Bristol Conference, in the year when his own father was President. Before he left Cambridge he had become Secretary of the East Anglia District Synod, and Probation Secretary for the Connexion, an office which he exercised most helpfully, and he preached far and wide in the village chapels of the circuit.

Another link with the Cambridge circuit had far-reaching effects in another direction. The Rev. G. R. Osborn, son of the dominating Dr George Osborn, came as Superindentent in 1884, and my father became engaged to his elder daughter. In those days Methodist rules forbade marriage till after ordination, but they enjoyed nearly twenty-five years of married life till my mother's comparatively early death in 1915, two months short of their silver wedding day. I owe my highest ideals of marriage to my boyhood memories of my father's attitudes to my mother. Even then I could sense his courtesy, his deep affection, and his sense of the holiness of the relationship. Though he took her death as a Christian man should, and continued to exercise in India the influence that he had always exerted, there was a gap in his life that nothing

15

could fill. The frequent references to my mother in his letters from India, though never morbid, show that all too clearly. When he died himself in the Mediterranean, there were (as his dear friend Rendel Harris put it) 'superior spiritual attractions' from the other side.

They had four children: Ralph, who was a Scholar of King's and Whewell Scholar in International Law, bidding fair to maintain the family traditions until he was killed in France in 1916, after his father had gone to India; Hope, whose death in Cambridge at the age of six was an abiding grief to her parents; myself, and my sister Helen. We are both now grandparents several times over. If only our parents and brother and sister could have had our length of life!

In 1902 came the move to Manchester, and the opportunity of a wider sphere of teaching. Though my father had had some brilliantly rewarding pupils at The Leys, and though he had lectured in Classics in the University, his real calling was to open the secrets of the New Testament to those who, like himself, were concerned with the ministry of bringing that Book into the minds and lives of men. This he did for thirteen years at Didsbury, and the tribute of his former students contained in this book are only samples of what all would say. By common consent his teaching was fascinating, human in all its scholarship, patient, and always enriching to the soul. Those adjectives are all W. F. Howard's, than whom no one is better qualified to judge, but everyone else would have agreed with them.

If mornings were given to the inspiring of the future Methodist ministry, many afternoons began with the rapid journey down to Manchester University. There he was Greenwood Professor in the Faculty of Theology, and for two years Dean; and he passed on to others belonging to different parts of the Church the same inspiration that he gave to his Didsbury men. In this sphere he was associated with his dear and eminent friend, A. S. Peake, and it was these two who made that Faculty the outstanding contribution to theological education that it has always remained.

In the last months of his life, when for a few weeks he was teaching Indian students in the United Theological College, Bangalore, he wrote a poem which shows his own attitude to the commission entrusted to him. It is called

At the Classroom Door

Lord, at Thy word opens yon door, inviting
  Teacher and taught to feast this hour with Thee;
Opens a Book where God in human writing
  Thinks His deep thoughts, and dead tongues live for me.

Too dread the task, too great the duty calling,
  Too heavy far the weight is laid on me!
O if mine own thought should on Thy words falling
  Mar the great message, and men hear not thee!

Give me Thy voice to speak, Thine ear to listen,
  Give me Thy mind to grasp Thy mystery;
So shall my heart throb, and my glad eyes glisten,
  Rapt with the wonders Thou dost show to me.

No wonder people 'heard him gladly', as men had heard his Lord. It was my own joy to teach for twenty-five years in that class-room where he had taught for those few weeks. I rarely entered its door without remembering something of his words, nor would any who heard him in Didsbury and in Manchester hesitate to assert that his Bangalore prayer had been answered every time he spoke to them.

As if all this teaching was not enough, there was incessant literary activity. His New Testament and Zoroastrian books are mentioned in the separate articles, but in addition there were *Visions of Sin* (studies of Bible characters published before he left Cambridge), the Fernley lecture for 1913 on *Religions and Religion* (a sympathetic but unhesitatingly Christian study of comparative religion, much of it written, as I well remember, in a hayloft on a Lakeland holiday, with occasional intermissions to feed the pony in the stable below), and two posthumous publications : *A Neglected Sacrament* (a collection of studies and sermons), and *The Christian Religion in the Study and the Street* (a collection of somewhat more academic papers though, it goes without saying, none of them are dry). Posterity must always be grateful to his brother, W. F. Moulton of Cliff College, for his work in collecting these two volumes, and for the very sensitive biography he wrote, its only fault being that war-time compelled it to be far too short.

Universities soon began to shower honorary doctorates on my father for his pioneer work in Hellenistic Greek. Edinburgh led the way, Durham and Groningen followed. Berlin was the latest, not long before the 1914 war broke out. Cambridge at that time did not give Divinity honours to Nonconformists. Yet he had interests more absorbing than honorary doctorates. He was deeply concerned with his friend S. F. Collier's Manchester Mission work and the intermingling of its evangelistic and social tasks. His acceptance of the Bible Society invitation to address its Annual Meeting was a symbol of the place that its work had in his thought. A visit to the West Indies on behalf of the Wesleyan Methodist Missionary Society was a token of his equal concern for the missionary task of the Church. He was an ardent Liberal, in the days when Liberalism was the most progressive element in politics, and he watched the beginnings of the Labour Party with keen sympathy. He would always be jumping up from the breakfast table to write a letter on a political or social concern to the

18

Manchester Guardian, unless the chair was being pushed back to verify a quotation from *Alice in Wonderland* or *Alice Through the Looking Glass*. He preferred the latter, primarily because he loved chess and hated cards! As for the Tory Party, a small boy gained the impression that there was something morally disreputable in belonging to it!

And with all this programme there was still time for games: croquet—a speedy variation—on our front lawn; tennis in the summer—he gave me my first lessons, as he did in Greek; golf now and then, and the hockey to which Mrs Harrison so delightfully refers.

War cast its shadow on these halcyon days. Didsbury was practically closed within a year. My mother died. And then, within a day or two of her funeral, came the invitation from Dr J. N. Farquhar on behalf of the Y.M.C.A to visit India and lecture to the Parsis in Bombay on their own religion. The invitation was a god-send. Missionary work had always been close to his heart. Academically his Zoroastrian and his New Testament work had been on a par with each other. He had delivered the Hibbert Lectures on *Early Zoroastrianism* in 1912. Now came the opportunity to meet the descendants of the Zoroastrians in person, to see and share in the work of the Church overseas, and to assuage to some degree the grief of my mother's death. My sister and I were left in the care of our uncle and aunt, who became second parents to us after his own death, and in October 1915 he sailed for Bombay.

The Rev. Frank Hart gives his picture of the time spent there. It was a time in which he endeared himself most deeply to the Parsis. Twenty or twenty-five years later they were still speaking of him to me. In the first instance it was his knowledge that impressed them. He knew more about their religion than they did! But even more it was his perfect courtesy. They knew that he was a Christian,

19

yet he never failed to respect their faith and to praise its values, and in an obituary notice one of them could say 'He died in our service'.

Yet, though the Parsis were the primary purpose of his visit to India, that visit spread well beyond its original intention. More time was spent in Bombay than in any other single place, but the circular letters written weekly during slightly under eighteen months indicate something like thirty-five changes of address. Although he writes consecutively for several weeks from Bombay, from Kotagiri in the Nilgiri Hills, and from the United Theological College, Bangalore, many more of the letters are written in long train journeys which took him anywhere from Darjeeling in the Himalayas to the south of Ceylon, half a continent away. Conferences, speaking engagements, and journeys to gain material for deputation work on his return to England, took him to Delhi, Agra, Hyderabad, Calicut, the Nilgiris, Mysore, Poona, Jabalpur, Colombo—names that are evocative to those who know India and Ceylon, and that indicate the vastness and wearisomeness of travel, especially in those days when there were no air services, and a moderate length journey from Bombay to Bangalore took thirty-six hours.

The Taj Mahal—a widowed husband's tribute to a beloved wife—moved him deeply. There was the terrible blow of my brother's death on the Somme. His own health was far from good—he overdid things as he had always done, and made little allowance for the demands of a tropical climate. There was much inner loneliness and great longing for letters from home.

Yet it was a deeply satisfying and enriching time, enriching for others even more than for himself. He made many friends, both among Indians and missionaries. He watched and learnt all the time everywhere. He gave

20

abundantly in all that he wrote, and spoke, and was. India exercised such a pull on him that he more than doubled the length of time originally planned for his visit, and for many reasons he would dearly have loved to stay on. It was a fitting climax to many aspects of his life : Zoroastrianism, missionary zeal, and his wonderful power of attracting and giving to all whom he met.

He sailed from Bombay in March on the 'City of Paris', and was joined in Port Said by his saintly Quaker friend, Rendel Harris, who had been torpedoed on the way out to India and had got no further than Egypt. The 'City of Paris' was torpedoed off Corsica, and though all on board got into the boats, and most got safely to land, the boat carrying Rendel Harris and my father missed its way. My father, troubled by boils and run down in health, toiled at the oars for three days until suddenly he went—on 7th April 1917.

Dr. Harris wrote the perfect letter about it all, a letter widely reproduced at the time. He told us of his courage and his thought for others, of those 'superior spiritual attractions' which lined the cloud of his going with gladness, of the many times when St Paul's words had been on his lips during the voyage, and of their shipboard conversation on Milton's Lycidas and the poignant significance that my father's own death at sea added to this last memory. These final days and hours were all of a piece with the rest of his life : poetry, friendship, the New Testament, the unseen world, and the taking of a towel and girding himself.

I have a book full of cuttings about him from many papers and magazines, religious and secular. In their different ways they all say the same things about his scholarship and character. Perhaps his obituary in the Minutes of Conference says them best :

'The greatness of his learning was matched by the depth

of his spiritual life and the beauty of his character. Warm-hearted and deeply devoted to Christ, he was an earnest and powerful preacher of His gospel, delighted in mission work at home and abroad, and had a passion for all that belonged to the Kingdom of God. An ardent social reformer, he joined eagerly in campaigns for public righteousness. He was full of brotherly love, simple and humble, ready to admire all who did great work, whether the scholars who were his peers, the students he taught, or the least known of his brethren in England or the mission field. He won from the whole Church a love as great as he gave.'

That is no mere official panegyric. It is how everyone who knew him felt about him.

H. K. MOULTON

His New Testament Work

NO PERIOD in New Testament textual and linguistic study has been more productive and stimulating than the time between 1881 and the first World War. It began with the publication of the Revised Version of the English New Testament and the Greek Testament of Westcott and Hort, two companion volumes which embodied the best work of the time and completed the process of breaking scholarship away from the so-called 'Received' Greek text of 1550 and the Authorized Version of the English New Testament, translated from it in 1611.

The fact that in certain directions scholarship has moved on since 1881 must not blind us to the wide-spread and exciting effect of these two volumes. On the one hand, they became the basis for scholarly New Testament work for the next half century and more. On the other, the English Revised Version became the normal book in Methodist pulpits, and the tradition in our home was that the servant, sent to bring the Bible for family prayers, returned with an Authorized Version, saying, 'I can't find the Bible, sir. Will this do?'

The other epoch-making event of the period was the realization by the young German scholar, Adolf Deissmann, that the language of some ordinary Greek documents written on papyrus paper, which he happened to be examining, was remarkably like the Greek of the New Testament. Others had had their suspicions of this, but the general opinion previously had been either that New Testament Greek was so debased that it should be avoided by all pure scholars, or that it was written in a special 'language of the Holy Ghost'. Deissmann's *Bible Studies,* published in German in 1895 and in English in 1901, changed the whole atmosphere by demonstrating that the New Testament, as

23

one would have expected, was written in the popular Greek of its own day, and that its vocabulary could be paralleled over and over again in letters, accounts and legal documents written by people who knew nothing of any New Testament writing. Hundreds of the familiar Biblical words and grammatical constructions were met with in entirely fresh contexts, which shed exciting new light upon them for their delighted discoverers.

I

My father came into this thrilling adventure very nearly at the beginning. All his previous academic work had been unconscious—or God-guided—preparation for his matching up with it. His Cambridge Tripos work had been in Indo-European Philology. His Dissertation on *Indogermanic Weak Aspirates,* a treasure which I still possess, shows a combination of maturity and originality scarcely credible in one who was still only twenty-two. Work of this nature was the foundation both of his later Zoroastrian studies, described in the next chapter, and of his New Testament grammatical and linguistic work, most of which remains indispensable to this day.

An equally valuable parallel training was provided by his close association with his father, William Fiddian Moulton, headmaster of The Leys School, Cambridge, from 1875 to his death in 1898. My father was first his father's pupil in the school. At the University he was still in his home town. As soon as he went down, he rejoined the school as a master and remained there till some years after his father had died. During this period my grandfather was one of the Revisers of the English New Testament and of certain books of the Apocrypha. It is easy to imagine the influence that this had upon a boy and young man whose natural bent was in this direction, whose brilliant mind took full advantage of all that he heard, and who had a devotion to his father bordering on reverence. For the Apocrypha panel B. F. Westcott and F. J. A. Hort were regular visitors to The Leys—I have a page of their autographs in the attendance register—and many others came to visit the father and prove at the same time an education to the son.

Even closer links with the Revised Version followed. As early as 1873, my grandfather was asked by the Revisers to be one of the two to undertake the preparation of the New Testament references. In fact the main work fell upon him, but owing to many claims on his time it proceeded slowly, and in his last years he received great assistance from his son and another old pupil, Dr A. W. Greenup. These two completed the task after his death, and went on to publish in 1910 *The New Testament with Fuller References,* on which W. F. Moulton himself had done a considerable amount of work.

Another link with the detailed study of the vocabulary of the Greek Testament was in connection with the Concordance planned by my grandfather in conjunction with A. S. Geden, and supervised by him throughout. My father had no direct connection with the initial preparation of this volume, but he worked through all the proof-sheets, and Mr. Geden acknowledges the 'scholarly care [which] has borne fruit on every page'.

One other influence remains to be mentioned. When W. F. Moulton's teaching career began—in the Wesleyan College at Richmond, Surrey—there was no satisfactory Greek New Testament Grammar in English. He therefore published a translation from the German of G. B. Winer's standard grammar, enriching it with many terse notes of his own, and providing such a valuable tool that it ran into three editions in twelve years. With the new discoveries of the 1890s, it became impossible for my father simply to revise it, as he had hoped. He had most reluctantly to abandon it and begin again, but his father's work had provided the foundation on which the new building could rise.

Philology, translation, concordance, grammar—it would be hard to plan a more adequate preparation for the life-work of a man such as my father; and if the bare titles sound somewhat dry, they were utterly redeemed by the personalities both of my grandfather and of his son. No two men could have combined more closely the character-istics both of accurate scholarship and of deep Christian devotion. Nor were these characteristics kept in separate compartments. The second grew naturally and reverently out of the first.

II

These then were the mental and spiritual qualifications which my father brought to meet the discoveries of the new era in New Testament studies.

Fortunately, both for his contemporaries and for posterity, he very soon began writing himself, and in 1902 he was appointed to Manchester, where he taught not only Methodist students in Didsbury Theological College, but many others in the newly-formed Theological Faculty in the University. The all too short period of twenty years' writing between 1895 and 1915, and of thirteen years' New Testament teaching from 1902 until he went to India, was as fertile as it could possibly have been. His influence on his students is described in other parts of this book.

His writing began while he was still at The Leys with the publication in 1895 of an *Introduction to the Study of New Testament Greek,* which was revised and developed by its author three times up till 1914, and still, with some further revision, remains one of the most widely used of beginners' grammars. It was my own joy to teach from it in India for twenty-five years. One typical characteristic of this clear and masterly book is a passage in the preface to the second edition where, after writing of the immense gain of reading the New Testament in the original tongue, he goes on to speak of his 'profound satisfaction when I found this book a few years ago in the hands of a poor and almost helpless cripple in a Black Country cottage. He had taught himself Greek enough to work through several chapters of St John, and he used the added knowledge of Holy Writ to instruct and inspire the young men who gathered around him in the little room which proved a very gate of heaven for many.' It was with aims such as this that my father did all his work, and any achievement of those aims was his deepest reward.

The small grammar, however, was only a beginning. A much larger project immediately began to take shape. It originated in his father's choice of him as his colleague for the complete re-writing of his edition of Winer's Grammar, mentioned above. The father died before a page of the new book was written, but the son took up the task, and in 1906 produced Volume I of his projected three volume *Grammar of New Testament Greek*, the *Prolegomena*. Rarely can a Greek grammar have made such a hit! To begin with, it dealt with a fresh and fascinating theme : the bearing of the new Egyptian discoveries on our understanding of the New Testament. To continue, it did so with scholarship of the highest order. To conclude, it was written in a style that was both clear and delightful. As Deissmann said in an enthusiastic review, 'One can really *read* Moulton'. Few grammarians would quote Sarah Gamp, remarking 'which her name is Mrs Harris', as a parallel to a Hellenistic idiom, or describe the Greek preposition ἐν as a 'maid-of-all-work'. It quickly ran into a third edition and has been reprinted several times since. It still sells over a hundred copies a year. It was even translated into German, a rare event for an English New Testament book in those days. The German translator left the sentence about Mrs Harris in the original, untranslated!

Volume II, on *Accidence,* was largely written but still in manuscript form when my father went to India in 1915. It was suspended while he turned his attention to Zoroastrianism, his second love, and was never resumed. It fell to his old pupil and friend, W. F. Howard, to complete it and see it through the press. This was done with great skill and devotion. Dr. Howard completed the Introduction with a most dexterous blending of other material from my father's published work and his own contribution which combines with it admirably. He also added the chapters on Suffixes and Semitisms which my father had planned, deservedly gaining his own doctorate from his work. No man could have done such a task more satisfyingly in every way.

Dr Howard had hoped to write Volume III on the Syntax but, to our great loss, he died too early in his retirement to have made much progress. Dr H. G. Meecham was then asked to undertake it, but death again stepped in. T. and T. Clark, the publishers, at last made arrangements with Dr Nigel Turner, and he has completed it this year.

III

While the Grammar was progressing, my father was engaged in another aspect of work on the Hellenistic vocabulary. He began with a series of Lexical Notes in *The Expositor,* but it was in this field that the new discoveries made themselves most fully felt, and there was obvious need for a full-scale volume, continuing systematically and in detail the work that Deissmann in his pioneer *Bible Studies* had begun. It would have to include alphabetically all the New Testament words to which parallels had been found in the papyri, and provide the student with the illustrations that would put the New Testament vocabulary in its cultural setting and illuminate his understanding of it by its general usage in its own time. The task of compiling the volume would be prodigious. In the end some three thousand words were illustrated, over a hundred collections of papyri and inscriptions were drawn upon, and over two hundred modern works of various kinds were consulted. It was a task beyond even my father's single powers, and he invited the Rev. Dr George Milligan, Regius Professor of Divinity in Glasgow, to co-operate with him. Together they published two parts of *'The Vocabulary of the Greek Testament, illustrated from the papyri and other non-literary sources'* before my father left for India. It remained for Milligan to produce the other six, but he was able to call throughout upon notes and references left by my father, so that in the end, when it was completed in 1930, it was all of it 'Moulton and Milligan', remaining both standard and fascinating until to-day. The General Introduction, finally written by Dr Milligan, is one of the clearest summaries of its subject to be found anywhere. And how much it helps, to quote only one example, to turn up the Greek word 'hēlikia', hitherto translated 'stature', and find that in current writing it normally meant 'maturity', 'age'. That makes sense of Matthew 6²⁵. Very few people want to be eighteen inches taller. Most, however, are desperately anxious to add to the length of their life. The R.V. margin was right here; it now has abundant contemporary evidence to support it.

The large grammar and 'Moulton and Milligan' were my father's major New Testament works. It has to be

29

remembered that he was cut off in his prime when only fifty-three. There were other shorter ones, however, of the same essential quality. There was his inaugural lecture as Greenwood Lecturer (later Professor) in Manchester University on *The Science of Language and the Study of the New Testament,* delivered in 1906 and reprinted in *The Christian Religion in the Study and the Street,* a collection of papers published posthumously by his brother, W.Fiddian Moulton, in 1919. This lecture is his own *credo* on the relationship between the two halves of its title. It finishes, as one would expect, with the hope that his students will 'find that grammar may become the minister of gifts which examinations cannot measure nor degrees certify'.

Then there was his contribution to *Cambridge Biblical Essays* (1909), entitled '*New Testament Greek in the light of modern discovery*'. In forty pages it covers his general field with much fresh detail, but perhaps the most interesting part of it is the central section dealing with the styles of the various New Testament writers. It was this section on which W. F. Howard wisely drew to complete the introduction to Volume II of the large Grammar.

In the original Peake's Commentary there were two contributions : an article on 'The Language of the New Testament', and the Commentary on James. In the new Peake, both have disappeared. In fact the new Peake, though an admirable volume, is not a revision of the old, as it claims, but an entirely new work. Like II Peter, it seeks to get its useful message home under a venerated name with which it has no connection except a common interest in the Christian faith !

My father's most popular book, however, was the series of five lectures delivered in Northfield, Massachusetts, in August 1914 and published by the Book-Room in 1916 under the title *From Egyptian Rubbish Heaps.* It ran into a second edition even in war-time. Much of his other work, readable though it was, had the scholar and the serious student in mind. This book opened the eyes of the 'ordinary' Christian to what was going on. In language that was at once scholarly, humorous and devotional, it showed him the papyrus discoveries, the force of the language of the New Testament, and the spiritual enrichment that these new studies could bring. Who that has heard or read it could forget the translation of Hebrews 11[1] and the comment on it? 'Faith is the *title-deeds* of things hoped for.' This is a sense in which the word usually translated 'substance' often occurs in the papyri, and my father draws the picture of the man with the title-deeds as the undisputable owner of the property, even if he has never seen it. 'If you look at the eleventh chapter of Hebrews, you will see that this is just what faith is there.' Not everyone has accepted this interpretation, but no one could fail to be enriched by the conception.

An illustration such as this might be said to sum up my father's whole approach to his chosen life-work. It was always based on the widest and most thorough scholarship, but it was not in his nature to let himself be entrapped by that caution which may lead to mental and spiritual stagnation. He was always eager to follow a speculation to its furthest legitimate limit, and to let his imagination work, without divorcing it from reality. Like his dear friend, Rendel Harris, he sometimes let in a great deal of light by daringly opening shutters, when others remained in the dark through keeping them cautiously closed. Yet there is never a hint of unsoundness in his work—only that spirit of calculated adventure by which all progress is made.

The illustration also exemplifies his deeply spiritual attitude to all that he wrote and said. He was first and foremost a Christian man, and his grammatical and linguistic studies were part and parcel of his essential Christian nature. He wanted to be objectively sure of the meaning of Hebrew 11[1], but he did not leave it as a piece of academic study. Those studies always led him and his readers on to the heavenly places in Christ Jesus.

IV

It is nearly half a century since his last New Testament work was written. How does scholarship regard it to-day? Dr Nigel Turner's article on 'The Language of the New Testament' in the new Peake's Commentary, which takes the place of my father's original article, is probably characteristic of much other opinion. It argues that my father and others 'may have gone too far at times in claiming that the N.T. language was simply the vernacular *Koine* of the period adapted to the needs of Christian disciples'. It stresses the influence of the 'Biblical Greek' of the Septuagint, both on the literary style and on the thought-content of the New Testament. It admits (with reservations) the value of the light shed on many obscure words by the papyrus discoveries, but points out that they leave us still in the dark with regard to words by which the Christian faith stands or falls. 'Study of papyri and literary Hellenistic authors must not be despised, but the rich rewards will come from Semitic study.'

I believe that my father would have welcomed comment of this nature. He had a mind that was eager to welcome all the new discoveries offered, but it was never closed against fair criticism. The progress of the Prolegomena illustrates this most fully. The first edition had nine pages of additional notes before it was published. The second had seven more, and the margins of his personal copy are besprinkled with pencilled jottings for future use. The third had a three page introductory note, calling attention both to major comments on previous editions, and to many minor changes made within the limits of the printed text. Many of these notes welcome new material supporting his themes, many correct freely-acknowledged errors, others are grateful for justifiable criticism. This attitude of mind would have persisted because it was part of my father's character.

At the same time he might have felt that, if he and others of his period were to be criticized for over-enthusiasm for the non-literary *Koine,* the pendulum is now in danger of swinging too far in the other direction. Granted that the papyri do not help us much with the great Christian words, there was no attempt to get more out of those documents than they can properly give. Granted that the Septuagint was strongly influenced by the idioms of the Hebrew Scriptures which it translated, and in its turn influenced the New Testament writers, this does not rule out the strong probability that all alike were influenced to a considerable extent both by the daily language spoken around them and by the more literary Greek styles of the day. The different proportions of this influence are very clearly recognised by my father in his sections on the styles of the New Testament writers. Granted also that more New Testament syntax is Hebraic than my father was inclined to admit, this does not mean that other influences are absent. Future scholarship may well adopt a more central position, willing to make greater allowance for the influence of the ordinary daily language of the people than Dr Turner will grant, while not perhaps going all the way with the claims of the early days of discovery.

Yet my father's old students would not want to leave the matter there. The testimonies in this volume, and all that have been given to me personally over the years, are built on a basis of the profoundest respect for his scholarship, but all go beyond that. They speak with delight of the times when he left the direct subject-matter of his lecture, the occasions when they led him, not unwilling, 'up the garden path', because it was always there that his choicest flowers were to be found. And, beyond even that, they knew that they would find in the class-room—as outside it—the humble, high-hearted, Christian man, who counted all his knowledge but a means to know more of his Lord and to impart Him to all who were willing to share in what he had found.

H. K. MOULTON

Zoroastrianism

IT SEEMS hardly possible that a man of my father's rank in New Testament studies could have found the time, let alone anything else, to attain almost equal rank in the apparently disparate field of Zoroastrianism. Yet the quantity and quality of his published work leave no doubt of the fact, and any record of his life and work would be incomplete without some account of his second great interest.

The link between the two subjects began with his study of Indo-European philology in Cambridge under E. B. Cowell, Professor of Sanskrit, who had taught Persian to Edward Fitzgerald and urged him to translate Omar Khayyam. Cowell's own humble Christian faith remained very different from the philosophy of the Persian poem, and my father gained from him the influence of a deeply Christian spirit as well as the connection of his Greek studies with their wider setting in other Indo-European languages. He dedicated to Cowell his first Zoroastrian book : *Early Religious Poetry of Persia* (Cambridge, 1911), inscribing it 'In piam memoriam Edward Byles Cowell *Tropheia*' (the wages due to a nurse). With Cowell he continued, long after undergraduate days, to read the Avesta, the sacred library of the ancient Persian religion. In the preface to his Hibbert Lectures he says that no pupil of Cowell's would omit to record his veneration for an ineffaceable memory.

As my father's knowledge of Zoroastrianism grew, his respect for it as a religious faith deepened. He often said that Zoroastrianism was the only non-Christian religion from which nothing needed to be subtracted, and that Christianity had only to add to it. The links between Persia and Palestine which began during the Jewish exile and continued into New Testament times are recognised by all Biblical scholars, though interpretations of the nature of mutual influence vary, but the title of my father's last book *The Treasure of the Magi* epitomises his belief that Zoroastrians, then as now, had things of great value to lay at the feet of the Christ who could enrich them still further. His whole attitude towards the relation between the two faiths is symbolized in the closing paragraph of the book, describing 'the parable written in the sky when in the early dawn he caught his first glimpse of India. A waning crescent moon hung over the harbour of Bombay and faintly illuminated the beautiful city that slept upon its shore. The borrowed radiance faded as the dawn drew on, and vanished, not destroyed but outshone, as the great sun leapt into the sky.'

My father's *Early Religious Poetry of Persia* is a small, though detailed, book of a hundred and seventy pages. He contributed articles on 'Fravashi' (a man's spiritual counterpart), 'Iranians' and 'Magi' to Hastings's *Encyclopaedia of Religion and Ethics*. But his major academic work in this field was his *Early Zoroastrianism*, the Hibbert Lectures for 1912, published by Williams and Norgate in 1913. This runs to a preface and four hundred and sixty-eight pages, and not only deals fully with history and beliefs but has evidence on almost every page of his power of looking at things with the eyes of the people about whom he is writing, and not merely from the dispassionate view-point of a modern scholar investigating the dead past. The acknowledgements in the preface show the wide range of his friendships : the American professor, A. V. Williams Jackson; the Roman Catholic Bishop Casartelli, his colleague in Manchester University, whose name I remember often on his lips; and his (as yet) pen friends among the Parsis in Bombay, whom he little thought that he would meet in the flesh two years after the book was published.

For it was in 1915 that my father's Zoroastrian work came to its climax. As recounted on page 21, he was able to accept the invitation of Dr J. N. Farquhar and visit India, primarily for the purpose of meeting and lecturing to the Parsis, descendants of the early Zoroastrians with whom he had been deeply concerned for so long, now migrated to Bombay and settled there and elsewhere in India to the number of about a hundred thousand. Though comparatively few in numbers, they are prominent in business and well-educated as a community, and they occupy positions in public life far in advance of their proportion to the total population. Mainly because of the smallness of their numbers, they have never felt that they could afford any leaks by way of conversion to other faiths. Such conversions have been few and far between, and have usually been the cause of considerable public agitation.

My father was sensitive to this attitude. Both his natural courtesy and his admiration for the Parsis' religion made him scrupulous in his respect, though he was always entirely frank in telling them that he believed that he had in Christ a possession that he dared not keep to himself. Having said this, he could challenge them to be better men by the standards of their own faith, in the belief that, the more truly they observed these, the nearer they would come to Christ. The very fact that he knew their religion so much better than most of them did lent authority to his words. His lectures were no mere academic exercises. They were a recall to religion, and a courteous, but very clear, Christian message. Eight of them have been collected and published by the Parsis themselves in a book entitled *The Teaching of Zarathushtra* (Bombay, 1917). They contain all the elements mentioned above : first-class scholarship, moral challenges based on Zoroastrianism as strong as those of any Hebrew prophet, frequent and effective reminders of the Christian faith and, as well, an expressed realisation that he is speaking to a community divided within itself, and a statement that he is not going to take sides. It is hard to see how his mission could have been better accomplished. There are still those who remember it with gratitude.

Dr Farquhar had asked my father, in addition to his lecturing, to write a book in 'The Religious Quest of India' series. This, *The Treasure of the Magi* (Oxford, 1917), was completed just before he left India on his final voyage. The original autograph went to the bottom in the Mediterranean, but the book was published posthumously from a type-written copy, the proofs being read and revised by Bishop Casartelli.

It is divided into two parts. The first is mainly a simpler and briefer survey of the Hibbert Lectures material. The second begins with the sentence 'Every visitor to Bombay finds out the Parsi before he has crossed the first street', and continues with personal observation on almost every page. One feels throughout the thrill my father had in linking years of academic study with living people practising a living faith. It is the same kind of thrill, evoked by places, that the classical scholar feels when at last he sees the Parthenon, or the man long conversant with the Bible when Jerusalem and Galilee are before his eyes. On the day after his arrival he was given the unique privilege of entering through the 'Parsis only' gate to witness the final stages of a Parsi funeral, before the corpse was taken up to the Tower of Silence. On another occasion a replica of one of the ceremonies of worship, lasting a whole hour, was specially performed for him by two of the priests. Personal discussions with reformers and with the orthodox were frequent, and there was much entertainment, gratefully accepted for the spirit in which it was offered and for the insights which it brought. All my father's academic writing would have been incomplete without this crown of personal contact.

There have been those who have found his estimate of Zoroastrianism too enthusiastic and too optimistic. Certainly in the forty-six years since his death there has been none of the moving forward to the Christian faith for which he longed. The Parsi is still the same dignified, friendly, immovable person that my father describes. Yet surely during these years it has increasingly been proved right to see the good in other faiths, and to be quite certain that evils are evils before denouncing them. Evils they may indeed be, but they may be no more than comparatively insignificant alternatives, with a spirit behind them that deserves the attempt to understand it. This was the attempt that my father made throughout. Some Christians have had nothing but contempt for 'heathen' religions. My father could write, 'I do long to see the Parsi faith what it was ages ago, a power to destroy all forms of evil and set up righteousness and loving-kindness and purity in the earth' (*Teaching of Zarathushtra,* p. 65).

Yet the last two chapters of *The Treasure of the Magi* show that there was no compromise whatever with the fundamentals of the Christian faith. While he could write with admiration of the work that Zarathushtra 'had so splendidly begun' (p. 219), he went on to write regretfully that the Parsi could not take the next step and see the uniqueness of Christ and the power of His Cross. Zarathushtra had a high doctrine of God: His unity, light, truth, holiness; but he knew almost nothing of God's love, that love revealed supremely in the Incarnation. He had a strong sense of good and evil, but thought too much in terms of merits and demerits, and the earning of reward or punishment. He knew nothing of the free salvation offered

39

to men who, whatever their degrees of goodness or badness, are in no position to save themselves.

After pages in which great deference is shown to Parsi teaching, and every effort made to find all that is good in it, my father sums up : 'What India needs, and all the world needs, is not a Teacher, nor even an Example, but a Life . . . . Of all the teachers of the Gentiles none has risen higher than Zarathushtra : only partially have any of them risen as high. The conspicuous failure of this great religion speaks eloquently of the supreme need of man. Vital energy, not precepts; power, not mere example; grace, not ideals—this is what our Christ gives, what every other messenger of God can only promise through Him' (p. 253).

Any Christian writer would make this claim. My father could make it with all the more right because years of penetrating, affectionate, understanding study had shown him so much that was good, and had left him still certain that in Christ the Parsis could have One who was better than any man's best.

H. K. MOULTON

As They Knew Him

IT WAS MY good fortune to meet James Hope Moulton when I was young. My father, John Simon, was Principal of Didsbury Theological College, near Manchester, and Dr Moulton came amongst us as a revelation and as a new kind of friend. I came from a family of militant Christians, but here came a scholar and a knight, so gentle as to inspire no sort of awe in young hearts. In fact, he was the making of our holiday hockey team and came swinging down the field to shoot a goal with unexpected accuracy and an equally devastating pun which left the defence in ruins. I can hear his high-pitched voice now, as he declared in triumph : 'This thing was not done in a corner.'

My father was wont to carry all before him in a different way. He loved battle and the skirl of the pipes, and when he sent out his students to preach, he chose for their commissioning the hymn which begins in that fine flourish of aggression, 'When Thy soldiers take their swords'. John Simon had never been known as one to suffer fools gladly. He met them with a broadside of sarcasm that his victims found difficult to appreciate. Now there is a law well known to the scholastic world that in every college there must be one perfect fool, and against such an unfortunate my father aimed his pretty turn of scathing wit in righteous indignation. He was disarmed in his battle charge and restrained by James Hope Moulton, who was an adept at beating swords into pruning hooks, with his suggestion that the culprit was 'a charming case of *sancta simplicitas*'. This large tolerance was a thing of wonder in the Didsbury of the fighting new Twentieth Century, and the poise of the scholar and the Christian a marvel not easily attained by the unlearned. As every college must have its perfect fool, it is well for every staff room if it possess both a Simon and a Moulton for the good of its soul.

At Didsbury there was no strife between James Moulton's beloved humanities and his science of religion, for they were as one, and both equally forbade him to call anything common or unclean.

It was from my father that I heard of Dr Moulton in the staff room, and from my husband that I learned of him in the lecture room. Archibald Harrison was his disciple and sat at the feet of James Moulton, in an Upper Room of lectureship, as the scholar unfolded the Greek New Testament to his students. So it came about that, as Archie Harrison bowed his head and buried the wrecks of humanity under Vimy Ridge in the First World War, he thought of Jamie Moulton and of the Bible's phrase of 'this vile body'. To his inner ear, in that hell of shot and shell, came a voice straight from Didsbury. It was pitched in unmistakable tone and it insisted on the right translation of those words from the Greek as 'the body of our humiliation'. Ever afterwards it was that translation and that airborne voice that wrapped themselves about the vileness as a gentle winding sheet for broken humanity.

It was the same to the end of James Moulton's life. When torpedoed, in that same war, and set adrift in the ship's boat of death, he ministered to the dark-coloured crew by drawing on his scholar's knowledge of Zoroaster. Thus he was able to commit them into their own God's hands, and that in their own language, when they came to die in the tragic unfriendliness of alien war. When his own time came, James Moulton followed them over the side into their World of Light, 'by the dear might of Him who walked the waves'.

It was typical of this scholar and saint that, when asked to introduce the new hymn-book to his Didsbury students, he should devote his lecture to the rejected hymns of the old book. The men could see for themselves what they had before them, but his heart, like his Master's, was yearning over the lost. There was one hymn for which he mourned especially, and those with eyes to see realized that the hymn was a transcript of the lecturer's own Christian experience, as he knelt in humility at the foot of the Cross. It was number Twenty-Four in the old 1876 *Collection of Hymns for the Use of the People called Methodists,* and it was by George Herbert. In his old copy Archie Harrison has written 'Omitted' and, for a man not given to exclamation marks, has followed up that word with *two* stalwart ones. The hymn reads :

> *Saviour, if thy precious love*
> *Could be merited by mine,*
> *Faith these mountains would remove;*
> *Faith would make me ever thine:*
> *But when all my care and pains*
> *Worth can ne'er create in me,*
> *Nought by me thy fulness gains;*
> *Vain the hope to purchase thee.*
>
> *Cease, O man, thy worth to weigh,*
> *Give the needless contest o'er;*
> *Mine thou art! while thus I say,*
> *Yield thee up, and ask no more:*
> *What thy estimate may be,*
> *Only can by him be told*
> *Who, to ransom wretched thee,*
> *Thee to gain, himself was sold.*

G. ELSIE HARRISON

*   *   *

THE PRIMARY memory of those whose listened for several years to one of the most outstanding scholars that God has given to Methodism is of the perpetual freshness of mind that was always there. 'Jimmy', as he was affectionately called, had no set lectures, repeated to successive generations of students. In his own studies he was always making fresh discoveries. He had been committed to the carrying out of the revision of the grammar of a language long since dead, and the labours of generations of scholars seemed to have left little promise of exciting new beginnings. But from the sands of Egypt there were coming masses of letters, official reports, bills etc., that were written in the Greek commonly used at the beginning of the Christian era and that was the language used by the writers of the New Testament.

This new evidence had to be sifted to discover the meanings of words and the grammatical forms current at the time. The immensity of the task is indicated by the thousands of references in all his works. In the class room we were not made conscious of the laboriousness of such an undertaking. Instead we were privileged to share in the excitement of the hunt being pursued with such zest, and morning by morning we listened to reports of the latest findings. The strictest canons of exact scholarship were unsparingly applied in examining the new evidence, but all was gladly done as the price for gaining new light on the meaning of the New Testament.

A fresh understanding of the uses of the tenses could give a clearer understanding of the working of God's grace. What evidence did they afford of God's act of saving? Was it something done once for all in one act? or was it repeated from time to time? or was it going on continuously, with completion somewhere in the future?

Or again, the proper assessment of the active and passive

forms of verbs had light to throw on some of the most significant words of Jesus. Was the eating of the bread and drinking of the wine an outward form to be observed? or was the emphasis on the activity of the mind in the observance of the form?

Moulton's continual showing of his own mind at work was characteristic of his method of teaching in all the branches of New Testament study in which he lectured. The evidence for a variant reading in the text was not just marshalled manuscript by manuscript. The scribes of Aleph and B and D, and even some of the correctors, became personalities capable of showing typical preferences. We were also led to recognize what Hort's judgement would be, and how an eccentricity would appeal to Rendel Harris.

While Moulton was highly scientific in his way of assessing evidence, emotion was never far away. A softening of the voice or the glistening of an eye would reveal his inner reaction to the suffering of the Cross, or to Christ's gentleness with children or a fallen woman. Records were not just cold facts but could speak of a love offered and accepted.

It may have been a weakness that so little time was devoted to formal instructions on set patterns, and that a wayward student could lead the discussion from an iota subscript to the consideration of the case of women's suffrage. But such weaknesses, if weaknesses they were, meant that we were able to share in the characteristic interests of a rich and gracious mind. We learned his scale of values. Sam Collier of the Manchester Mission excited his admiration and almost envy. We often felt that he would gladly have surrendered his ability as a scholar for the power to speak of his Saviour to the common man as Collier did.

He had a keen appreciation of the truth to be found in

non-Christian religions, but this made him the more aware of the fulness to be found in Christ. Missions were for him an essential part of the Church's life.

His books show him to be a scholar with a creative genius, but his self-revelation in the class-room fashioned the minds of men. Some he made into scholars, others into evangelists, others into missionaries. He taught all to be gentle with the weak and the young and, above all, to love and serve with zeal the Lord who was his own Master.

A. H. BRAY

*　　*　　*

MY FIRST recollection of Dr James Hope Moulton was when I came up as a candidate for the ministry to Didsbury College to take an examination. This was in the lecture room in which later Dr Waddy Moss poured out breathlessly the contents of his well-worn theological notes. In the course of the examination Dr Moulton came in to see the examiners, bringing a breath of fresh air. I had no idea who he was, but gathered that he was a person of some importance. I do remember being impressed by his voice, which was very high-pitched and had a kind of rippling sound. He spoke very rapidly, but quite distinctly.

I am afraid that my own personal interviews with the doctor were few and far between. This was not because he was in any degree unapproachable, but because my studies in Hellenistic Greek never warranted any demands upon his time. I do, however, remember a visit to his house after preaching in the college chapel, to hear his criticism of my sermon. He on his part seemed to regard it as a kind of impertinence to pass judgment on a man's preaching. He was very come-at-able and charming, and certainly let me off lightly. 'Rather rhetorical', was the nearest to adverse criticism that he made; and then, as though fearing to frighten Timothy, he added, 'but very good rhetoric'! On another occasion when I called on him for a subscription for something, I was no sooner over the doorstep than he suddenly appeared. He seemed to have a way of appearing suddenly. He was always quick and darting in his movements, for ever on his way to an engagement. On this particular evening he was evidently about to fulfil an important appointment, for he was wearing a dress suit. Unfortunately, in shaving too rapidly he had cut himself badly, and was staunching the wound with his pocket handkerchief, doing his best to talk to me between the jabs at his cheek.

It was in his lecture room that he came to his own for us. There, sitting at his feet, we learnt to know something of his great wealth of learning and culture. We discovered as well some of his foibles and a few weak places in his armour. There was in him a beautiful naivety—not childishness, but unselfconscious childlikeness which came out in all sorts of ways. He was transparent as glass, and how ashamed one feels to have ever taken advantage of his fine humility .

Dr Moulton—'Jimmy', as we called him—would appear at the last moment at the door of his lecture room as one caught up and blown in by the winds of heaven. There was indeed something almost birdlike in his appearance and movements—if one has in mind the noblest of wild birds, the eagle. Perched in his eyrie or desk, he would take a swift glance round at his pupils and then perhaps suddenly pounce upon an offender. 'Oh, Mr Blink, you've come without your Greek grammar. Come without your collar and tie if you like, but always bring your Greek grammar.'

In our year there were a number of dullards like myself. When it came near to the turn of one of these, he would likely come out with some such irrelevance as, 'Oh Doctor, I went to the Church of the Holy Name on Sunday and . . .' The wily one was not allowed to go further. 'Ah,' said our teacher, 'I know them . . .' The back boys breathed freely again for, once started off on another trail, they knew that a very interesting contribution would flow freely from him until the bell rang.

Looking back, one reflects that we were not the clever ones, but had really been out-manoeuvred by one who knew our capacities, or lack of them, far better than we did ourselves. Dr Moulton no doubt realized that no one can teach Greek; it can only be caught by those of the right tinder. Here, he knew, were men going out into circuit life, having to speak to people, many of whom were on the same level as the ignoramus quoted by him, who asked, 'Did Paul know Greek?'

Perhaps then the greatest debt I owe to Moulton is that he exemplified in character and life the glorious liberty of the sons of God. There was no envy or pettiness about him, such as sometimes spoils a minister's career. There was a freshness and vitality about him that swept away the stuffiness of a Methodism existing for itself. James Hope Moulton for me represented the Christian man as the soldier-saint. If in his crusading for the emancipation of women, or for missions, we did not always see their relevance for the Methodist ministry, it was only to realize later, because of his example, the meaning of religion and life. How far sighted he was! When I first came to Didsbury, motor cars were something novel, but when someone mentioned their growing popularity, he quietly observed that they might not prove an unmixed blessing to poor people living in villages. Also he warned us of very difficult days ahead. This was some years before the first World War.

In James Hope Moulton, intellect and emotion were finely balanced. It was his tenderness and sensitivity that impressed us most. Often, in expounding a passage of Scripture, he would refer to 'my dear father', and never without a rising of the Adam's apple in his throat and something near a sob. Some of his students were not always as sympathetic as they should have been. One of them, I remember, reproduced the emotional moment in a rather different context. It was at the time when Moulton had published his 'Prolegomena'. The student in question vividly imitated the agitation and distress of his beloved tutor rushing into the study, wringing his hands, and crying, 'Oh dear! Oh dear! What shall I do? My dear little boy has swallowed my Prolegomena!'

Caricatures, of course, but a man has to become a Somebody before he becomes the subject of a cartoon. The yearly concert was hailed as a suitable outlet for youthful levity. It was graced by the presence of the Governor and members of the tutorial staff. Following a number of rather frivolous items, we found it a little difficult to compose ourselves to the right mood for an item from 'Elijah'—'If with all your hearts ye truly seek Me'—sung by our beloved tutor in a rather high falsetto voice.

A pet aversion of the doctor's was tobacco. It was grounded, I think, not in puritanical prejudices but in hygienic reasons. When about to entertain a number of university students, he so far waived his prejudice as to go into a tobacconist's shop. 'I want some cigarettes,' he said politely. 'What kind, sir?' enquired the man at the counter. 'Oh, is there more than one kind?' came the surprised answer.

Moulton may have been a man of strong feeling. Our

Lord, we are told, was a man of strong passions, but emotion for Him became compassion. Similarly with His servant James Hope Moulton. He was of compassion compact! A close friend of mine had been 'put back for two years' for breaking an unfortunate engagement. I met him as he came away from the Discipline Committee. X was naturally very cut up but, slipping his arm through mine, he said, 'Bodgie, Dr Moulton has behaved like a brick. Do you know, he came to me with tears in his eyes, and spoke to me in a way I shall never forget.'

These notes cannot convey my deep and abiding admiration for one who, in whatever calling he might have followed, could not be less than a fine English gentleman. It was much to sit daily at the feet of one who embodied the best of English breeding and culture. It was more to discover in him a speaking likeness of Mr Valiant-for-Truth. It was much more, to one student at least, to see reflected in his life, his teaching and his actions an image of the Jesus of the Gospels. His one-time student now writing can say with no exaggeration that he not only loved this great man but approached as near to worship of him as a man may go in his devotion to another, this side of idolatry.

J. H. BODGENER

*   *   *

THERE ARE some privileges which come to us in life which we do not appreciate until they are past. Amongst them I would place the tuition we received from one of the greatest scholars of our age, and one of the humblest, Dr James Hope Moulton. His tall athletic figure, alert, using every minute to the best advantage, his personal interest and patience with us in our fumblings and stumblings in New Testament Greek—these are things that one recalls with deep thankfulness that such a privilege was ours.

He was always in a hurry, but that was due to the careful way he planned out every minute to make the best use of it. Hastening along the corridor to his classroom, he would arrive a minute before time. Ringing the bell vigorously we assembled for his class. At the close of his morning's session, back he would hasten to his home, then off to the university to lecture in the afternoon—and so on.

One Saturday afternoon he was hastening from Manchester Central station to Victoria to catch a train to fulfil his Sunday appointment. As he passed the Town Hall, he met two little children sobbing their hearts out. He stopped and tried to find out the trouble. They were lost. So he took their hands, led them to the Albert Hall, handed them over to the Sister in charge, and asked her to see that they were fed, cared for, and 'found'. Then he went to the nearest telegraph office and wired that he was coming by a later train.

These week-end appointments usually brought some comments on the Tuesday when classes recommenced, and fortunate were the ones who had the first session. It was the custom in those days to have an 'Open Forum' with questions invited from the congregation at the close of the evening service. 'Really,' said Dr Moulton, 'I didn't think people could be so ignorant.' We waited expectantly. 'A man asked me how it was possible for someone to have *FOUR* mothers. I said to him, "Whatever do you mean?", and he said, "It says in the Bible that a man was born of four".'

There was a lovely naive simplicity about him, for instance with regard to terms which came into general use

51

in the first World War: 'Platoon, platoon . . . I thought that was what soldiers crossed rivers on.'

He taught us to love our New Testament, and to love our Lord; and he was to us the expression of a Christian minister fully dedicated in mind, heart and will to the service of Christ.

J. O. COCHRAN

*   *   *

WHEN I SAW the announcement of classes in Hellenistic Greek at Manchester University, to be conducted by Dr Moulton, I wrote asking if I could attend them and if I ought to know more Greek than I did to be able to appreciate them. He replied saying that I should be welcome to attend, and that probably some students would know more Greek and some less than I did. I am quite sure that I did know less than the others, but never at any time did he make me conscious of this. All the same, when I listened to him and found how important it was to understand points of Greek grammar, such as tenses and cases, in order to see the fascinating way these affected the texts we were studying, I used to walk across the quad to catch my tram, determined to give my mind to learning Greek grammar more thoroughly in order to follow what he said.

At the same time it was not necessary for me to take all the grammatical details quite as seriously as the others did, who were theological students with their B.Ds. looming before them, so I must confess that my pen was most vigorous when the Doctor indulged in his frequent and illuminating asides and diversions. The other students used the opportunity to relax!

Once, when we were beginning Hebrews, he did em-
barrass me by looking at me and suddenly asking, 'Now
why should *you* know who wrote Hebrews?' I had been
brought up on the orthodox view that nobody knew who
wrote Hebrews, and was non-plussed. Why should *I* know?
I thought of Paul and Apollos and so on, till the Doctor
cut short my embarrassment by saying, 'Why, of course,
because it was probably written by Priscilla!' My embarrassment was quite forgotten at such a thrilling, hitherto
unheard-of proposition.

Dr Moulton used to make us feel in touch with the other
great scholars of the time. He would say, 'I've just had a
letter from Dr Deissmann, (or Dr Milligan, or Dr Ramsay),
so that we felt right in the foreground of up-to-date interpretation of the Bible. His lectures contained innumerable
references to the Scriptures, the Classics, English literature,
and the writings of other faiths. Matthew Arnold, he might
tell us, said so and so, and we should find the same idea in
Zoroaster, and of course Plato came very near it in such
and such a dialogue, and undoubtedly Leviticus in chapter
so and so and verse so and so is a reference to the same
thought. He dived about in the literature of all periods.
Among other faiths his references to Zoroastrianism were
the most frequent. For instance, in explaining the phrase
in Revelation : 'the angel of the church', he said that all
sorts of suggestions had been made. 'Some have thought it
meant the bishop—it being assumed, I suppose, that bishops
are always angels! But that won't work. A different kind
of angel is meant, and this idea comes in Zoroaster. The
angel is the heavenly counterpart of a person—a definite
part which dwells in heaven and is united with the soul
at death. When Christ, speaking of the children, says, "In
heaven their angels are always beholding the face of my
Father who is in heaven", he endorses this view. In this

case the angel belongs to one who has not sinned, and is therefore always in the presence of God from whom sin would separate him.'

Commenting on John 3[11] : 'We speak of what we know', the Doctor explained that nothing original in connection with religion was tolerated by the Jews of our Lord's day. The teaching of Jesus, coming straight from God, they would not listen to; it had no credentials. So their own writings took shelter under some great name, such as Enoch or the Testimony of the Patriarchs. 'I needn't add,' said he, 'that the lofty character of the teaching in some of these works would have considerably astonished the Patriarchs themselves!'

Speaking about the healing of the blind man in John 9, the Doctor said that Sabbath observance meant so much to the Jews that when they saw the man who had been blind the only thing they stopped to ask was, 'What day of the week was it?' And commenting on Luke 13[10] he said, 'This woman had been ill for eighteen years. Could she not have waited another day? Yes, *she* could, *He* couldn't. She gave Him the opportunity of discountenancing the Pharisaic observance of the Sabbath, and He took it.'

Dr Moulton disagreed with people who said that the parable of the Prodigal Son was incomplete because it left out the idea of atonement. 'We must ask,' he said, 'what effect the treatment of the father had on the prodigal. It must have produced a vital amendment all through his life, and there you have the essence of atonement. The Father's love enters into a man's soul and transforms it.'

The Doctor's many-sidedness was shown in his willingness to strike a blow for causes that he cared about. He was a whole-hearted supporter of the Suffragist movement, and on one occasion had been asked to address a meeting which immediately followed our class. I also was going to the meeting, so we took the tram into Manchester and talked about the things we had just been discussing in class. At the meeting he went on to the platform, and then the fun started. A contingent of Suffragettes was there, come to heckle. They immediately attacked the Doctor; he enthusiastically counter-attacked, and there was some uproar. From the studious atmosphere of a tiny room at the university, with some half-dozen of us immersed in points of Hellenistic Greek, to the bawling mass of a Women's Suffrage meeting in Manchester was a change of atmosphere, to put it mildly. Yet both were typical of Dr Moulton. Wherever he could be of help to any cause he believed in, there he went, and that immediate response was especially conspicuous in his last missionary journey.

For all of us who were fortunate enough to study under him, he was indeed the beloved Doctor.

DORIS HURST

*　　*　　*

DR MOULTON came to Bombay in 1915 to take up a Readership in the university, and to make a personal study of the Parsi community. At a civic welcome in the Town Hall, the Parsi leader, Sir Ratan Tata, said, 'We are delighted to see Dr Moulton, and honoured to have him in our city. He is a great scholar, a revered teacher and, in this troubled time, a messenger of peace.'

The European war had brought discredit on the Christianity of the churches, and Christian missions were being confronted by a Hinduism long passive, gathering its forces to resist. In the Parsi community there was unrest, with voices calling for reform to sweep away old rituals and meaningless words. The Christian Church was weakened by its own divisions.

Dr Moulton did more than he knew to unite the Christian forces and to strengthen the Christian witness. There was an instant response from Indians at the mention of his name. He gave hours of thought and prayer to his lectures, and delivered them without a note. His gentle spirit and serenity of mind, his tolerance and unfailing courtesy impressed his hearers. His lectures and addresses were memorable not only for the grasp and range of his scholarship, and his high conception of the scholar's task. He conveyed also through them his experience of God in Christ, and the vastness of His grace. This gave them their extraordinary quality and immediacy. Not only his words but his heart spoke. All his utterances were a harmonious contribution to one great end : to make the Name of Jesus known and loved among all men. 'The Magnitude of His Name' was the subject of his last service in India. From the platform I listened as a learner enthralled by a master, seeing in the faces of the audience something of the profound impression Dr Moulton made upon his hearers. The experience of being with him is a purifying influence after nearly fifty years.

On the occasion of his lecture to the university, Sir Narayan Chandavarkar, the Vice-Chancellor, welcomed him as a scholar of international fame, a master of the masters in his own subjects. His lecture was acclaimed by the press as one of the deepest utterances in the history of the university. He spoke later at the University Settlement to Indian women in training, and to the Queen Mary High School for Girls, chiefly Parsis. He addressed also the staff and students of Wilson College, and the Y.M.C.A. classes frequently. The Brahmin leaders of the Prathana Samaj (the Prayer Society) invited him to speak at their Sunday evening gathering in the city. As he entered the room, he saw, woven on a silk scroll, the words 'The Kingdom of God is within you,' and he spoke from these words of Jesus as 'His sovereign light within my heart'.

K. T. Natarajan, editor of the *Indian Social Reformer,* wrote of Dr Moulton's influence upon the Indian mind. In conversation he added, 'It was his humbleness of heart which led more than one to the feet of Christ'. There were black sheep too in the English fold who found through him the homeward way.

The Parsi leaders told him of the unrest in their community, and how they lacked spiritual food. They asked him to give five lectures on Saturday afternoons in a theatre in the city, an opportunity which he accepted with joy. He spoke of them as 'Gospel Sermons from Zoroastrian Texts'. 'For the Parsis Jesus Christ came not to destroy but to fulfil. Everything that is beautiful in Zarathushtra's teaching has its completeness and crown in Christ, beyond all that he dreamed.' Dr Moulton had shown them where to find spiritual food.

In thanksgiving the Parsis invited him to enter the Tower of Silence, where the dead are exposed to the vultures, and the chief Fire Temple in Bombay, to see the sacred fire which perpetually burns, and which normally Parsis alone are permitted to view.

His own memorial service in the Methodist Church in Apollo Bunder was attended by many Hindus, including Sir Narayan Chandavarkar, and by many more Parsis, with Dr J. J. Modi, the old and honoured head of the community. He said, 'Dr Moulton taught us more of our religion than we ourselves knew.'

He gave himself without reserve to our missionaries. His daily letters to them were a real part of his ministry in India, full of affection and personal interest in their families and their work. He travelled far to see them. He came close also to the outcastes in the Marathi Mission and saw how Christ touched them through the hands of their minister, Samuel Rahator. He saw too in Benares the marvellous change in the lives of the Doms. His heart was drawn to them as by a magnet. A lean-to of grass matting over a mud floor, and a dozen children of the untouchables saying the Lord's Prayer, remained his deepest memory of India.

By midsummer 1916 there were six thousand beds in Bombay for sick and wounded men from Mesopotamia and East Africa. Dr Moulton, in his own deep sorrow caused by the loss of his wife shortly before he arrived in India, volunteered for service among these men. He cycled round, carrying 'Comforts', and spent hours in the wards. His visits were blessed both to Indians and to British. How often men asked, 'Who was the gentleman who came round the other day?' One of his countrymen, who had many wounds, said, 'He helped me to realize that Christ is sharing my pain.'

Two memories of this beloved friend are deeply hallowed. One is when he asked me to join him at the piano in singing Wesley's evening hymn. 'Omnipresent God, whose aid No one ever sought in vain'. He had heard the day before of the death of his brilliant son Ralph on the Somme, and this was the hymn Ralph had asked for on the eve of his going to France. The other was when, tired and suffering from boils, he was leaving India. We knelt in his cabin. He prayed and, when he ceased, we remained on our knees. In the hush Christ was so near that I felt if I moved I might touch Him.

FRANK HART

*   *   *

'As THEY knew him'—that, for me, was as a little girl knows a much loved father. He had gone before I had the opportunity of more mature knowledge. That has come to me since and in many ways, through his writings and through contacts with others who knew him. Yet I realize, as I look back over the years, what a deep impression he made on me and how much of his teaching and example have stayed with me all through my life. Little incidents come to my mind, perhaps too trivial to be given the importance of the printed word, and yet I think they serve to illustrate facets of his character which may not have been touched upon in other parts of this book.

His gifts in the lecture room need no emphasizing by me, but he could teach a small child too, and what little knowledge I have of astronomy was gained at a very early age when he would come to fetch me from some children's party and make the walk home an enthralling delight as he pointed out the constellations : Cassiopeia, the Pleiades, Orion, Scorpio and many more—names that sounded wonderful to a six or seven-year-old, and that have never been forgotten.

Thunderstorms, often so frightening to the very young, were to me something to be looked forward to, for at the first rumble of thunder, in the evening when I had gone to bed, Father would come hurrying up the stairs and stay with me until the storm was over, by his presence taking all the fear away.

Mention has already been made by others of his keen interest in a wide range of subjects that led him to use every moment of the day to the full. I smile as I remember how his urgency once cost him a damaged jacket and a sore shoulder. He was returning home from the station at Didsbury and, on leaving the station entrance, instead of following the pathway skirting the curve of the station yard, he took the short cut straight across. In those days the horse cabs used to line up round the curve and, in order to take the short cut, my father ducked between the nose of one of the horses and the back of the cab in front. The horse took exception to this rather startling behaviour, bent down, and nipped him! I rather imagine that he received a scolding from my mother on his return home!

Two lessons I learnt very early in life, and directly from him, were the care of books and the care of the country-side. I came to feel that to ill-treat a book was almost as bad as to ill-treat an animal or a child, and to this day, whenever I see a book being mishandled, I immediately have a mental picture of my father, so well did he instil the lesson into me. As for the countryside, I often think how pained he would be, could he see the work of the modern litter lout, especially in this land of Australia where I now live. Whenever we went for picnics on our summer holidays, every sign of our temporary occupation of a site had to be removed before we left. I can visualise very clearly helping him to dig a hole under some bushes in a remote Welsh valley in order to bury the rubbish, and then smoothing the earth neatly into place afterwards, so that no one would know we had been there. These lessons have become so much a part of my make-up that they have been faithfully passed on to my children and grand-children.

These and other little incidents are perhaps of small significance in a life such as his, full as it was of much bigger things. Yet they show that, in the fullness of his life and the greatness of his many gifts, he still had time to be what is, after all, one of the greatest gifts—a wonderful father.

HELEN HOPE HOLLINGS